Disabilities and Differences

We All Read

Rebecca Rissman

Heinemann Library
Chicago, Illinois

Customer Service 888-454-2279
Visit our website at www.heinemannlibrary.com

Printed and bound in China by South China Printing Company Limited

13 12 11 10 09
10 9 8 7 6 5 4 3 2 1

Library of Congress Cataloging-in-Publication Data
Rissman, Rebecca.
 We all read / Rebecca Rissman.
   p. cm. -- (Disabilities and differences)
 Includes bibliographical references and index.
 ISBN 978-1-4329-2154-5 (hc) -- ISBN 978-1-4329-2160-6 (pb) 1. Reading--Juvenile literature. I. Title.
 LB1050.R55 2008
 428.4--dc22
                       2008030378

Acknowledgments
The author and publisher are grateful to the following for permission to reproduce photographs: ©agefotostock pp. 19 (John Birdsall), 22 (Banana Stock); ©Alamy p. 20 (David Lyons); ©Corbis pp. 9 (Paul Barton), 12 (zefa/Brigitte Sporrer); ©drr.net pp. 10 (Brett Snow), 18 (Anderson Ross), 21 (Design Pics/ Kristy-Anne Glubish); ©Getty Images pp. 4 (Tay Rees), 6 (Jose Luis Pelaez Inc.), 7 (Image Source), 8 (Abid Katib), 15 (China Photos), 16 (AFP PHOTO/LIU Jin), 23 middle (Abid Katib), 23 bottom (China Photos); ©Ladov pp. 14 (REUTERS/Crack Palinggi), 23 top (Reuters/Crack Palinggi); ©shutterstock pp. 11 (Jose AS Reyes), 13 (Nir Levy), 17 (Matka Wariatka).

Cover image used with permission of ©Landov (Xinhua). Back cover image used with permission of ©drr.net (Anderson Ross).

Every effort has been made to contact copyright holders of any material reproduced in this book. Any omissions will be rectified in subsequent printings if notice is given to the publisher.

Contents

Differences

We are all different.

Reading

We read words.

We read sentences.

We read to learn.

We read to laugh.

How We Read

People read in different ways.

People read in different places.

Some people read from left to right.

Some people read from right to left.

Braille

Some people read with their fingers.

headphones

Some people use sounds to help them read.

character

Some people read characters.

Some people read letters.

What We Read

Some people read books.

Some people read newspapers.

Some people read signs.

Some people read computers.

We Are All Different

We are all different.
How do you read?

Words to Know

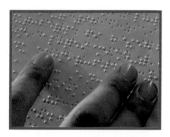

Braille raised bumps on paper. People read Braille with their fingers.

glasses small pieces of glass worn over the eyes. Glasses help some people see.

headphones small speakers worn over the ears. Some people use headphones to help them read.

This section includes related vocabulary words that can help students learn about this topic. Use these words to explore reading.

Index

Note to Parents and Teachers
Before reading
Discuss with students what it means to be different. Then, explain that we can have things in common, too. Tell children that our similarities and differences are both important.

After reading
Ask students to think of their favorite story. Have each child draw a book cover for the story. Then, ask students to form small groups or partners to share each cover and story.